CONTENTS

GEORGE GERSHWIN was born in Brooklyn on September 26, 1898, and began his musical training when he was 13. At 16 he quit high school to work as a "song plugger" for a music publisher and soon he was writing songs himself. "Swanee," as introduced by Al Jolson, brought George his first real fame and led to his writing a succession of 22 musical comedies, most with lyrics by his older brother, Ira. The Gershwins' shows include *Lady, Be Good!; Oh, Kay!; Strike Up the Band; Girl Crazy;* and the Pulitzer Prize-winning *Of Thee I Sing.* From his early career George had ambitions to compose serious music. These ambitions were realized in some of his masterpieces of American music, among them "Rhapsody in Blue," "Concerto in F," "An American in Paris" and "Second Rhapsody." In the late '20s George became fascinated by the DuBose Heyward novel *Porgy,* recognizing it as a perfect vehicle for opera using jazz and blues idioms. George's "folk opera" *Porgy and Bess* opened in Boston on September 30, 1935, and had its Broadway premiere two weeks later. In 1937 George was at the height of his career. In Hollywood, working on the score of *The Goldwyn Follies,* he collapsed and on July 11 died of a brain tumor. He was not quite 39 years old.

IRA GERSHWIN , the first songwriter to be awarded the Pulitzer Prize, was born in New York City on December 6, 1896. In 1917 *The Evening Sun* published his first song lyric ("You May Throw All the Rice You Desire But Please Friends, Throw No Shoes"). Four years later Ira enjoyed his first major stage success, *Two Little Girls in Blue,* written with another Broadway newcomer, Vincent Youmans. In 1924 Ira and his brother, George, created the smash hit *Lady, Be Good!* and went on to continue their remarkable collaboration through a dozen major stage scores, producing such standards as "Fascinating Rhythm," "The Man I Love," "'S Wonderful," "Embraceable You," "I Got Rhythm," "But Not for Me" and others far too numerous to mention. During his long career, Ira also enjoyed productive collaborations with such composers as Harold Arlen, Vernon Duke, Kurt Weill, Burton Lane and Jerome Kern, with whom he created his greatest song hit of any one year, "Long Ago and Far Away." Ira Gershwin died on August 17, 1983, in Beverly Hills, California.

CRAZY FOR YOU is the musical story of Bobby Child, a rich, pampered, 1930's New York playboy who is sent by his domineering mother to Deadrock, Nevada, to foreclose the mortgage on a long-dormant theatre. Upon arrival in the lazy Western mining town, Bobby's adventures take an unexpected turn when he falls head-over-heels in love with Polly Baker, the only girl in a town of 157 men.

The high-energy comedy of **CRAZY FOR YOU**, directed by Mike Ockrent and choreographed by Susan Stroman, is played out in song, high-stepping dance numbers and fast-breaking plot twists in the best Broadway "boy-gets-girl" tradition, where everybody's in love with the wrong person.

K-RA-ZY FOR YOU

Music and Lyrics by
GEORGE GERSHWIN
and IRA GERSHWIN

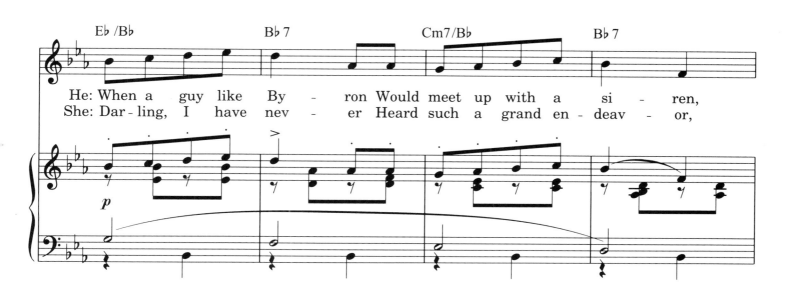

He: When a guy like By-ron Would meet up with a si-ren,
She: Dar-ling, I have nev-er Heard such a grand en-deav-or,

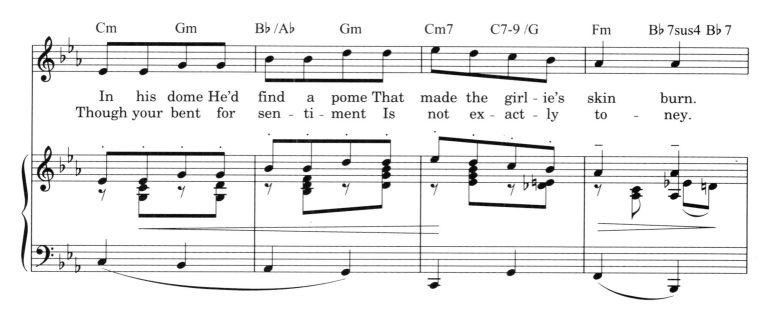

In his dome He'd find a pome That made the girl-ie's skin burn.
Though your bent for sen-ti-ment Is not ex-act-ly to-ney.

I CAN'T BE BOTHERED NOW

Music and Lyrics by
GEORGE GERSHWIN
and IRA GERSHWIN

BIDIN' MY TIME

Music and Lyrics by
GEORGE GERSHWIN
and IRA GERSHWIN

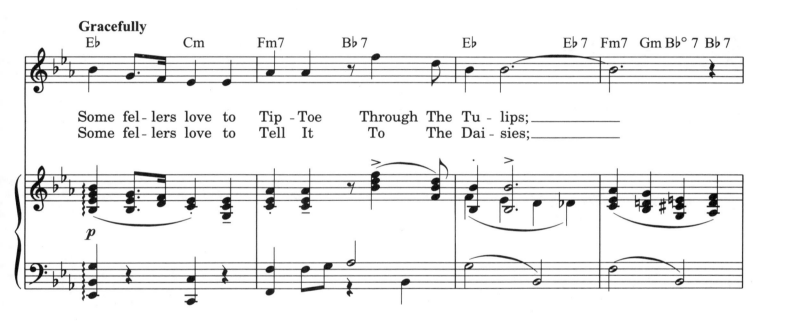

Some fel-lers love to Tip - Toe Through The Tu - lips;____
Some fel-lers love to Tell It To The Dai - sies;____

Some fel-lers go on Sing - ing In The Rain.____
Some Stroll Be-neath The Hon - ey-suc-kle Vines;____

THINGS ARE LOOKING UP

Music and Lyrics by
GEORGE GERSHWIN
and IRA GERSHWIN

COULD YOU USE ME?

Music and Lyrics by
GEORGE GERSHWIN
and IRA GERSHWIN

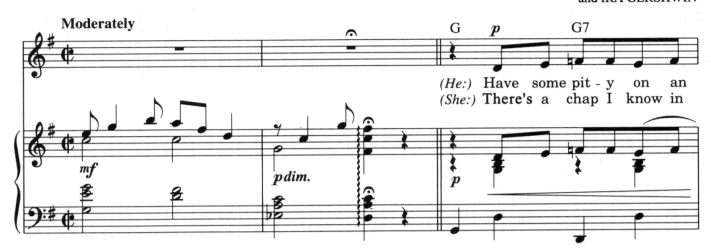

SHALL WE DANCE?

Music and Lyrics by
GEORGE GERSHWIN
and IRA GERSHWIN

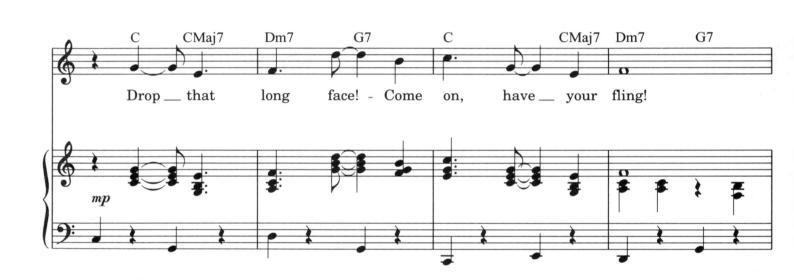

SOMEONE TO WATCH OVER ME

Music and Lyrics by
GEORGE GERSHWIN
and IRA GERSHWIN

SLAP THAT BASS

Music and Lyrics by
GEORGE GERSHWIN
and IRA GERSHWIN

Zoom - zoom!__ zoom - zoom!__ The world is in a mess! With

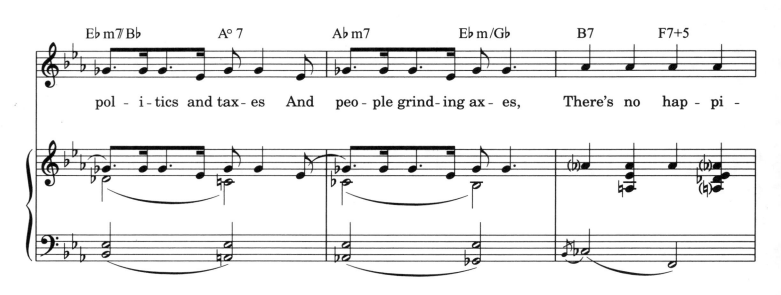

pol - i - tics and tax- es And peo - ple grind- ing ax- es, There's no hap - pi -

EMBRACEABLE YOU

Music and Lyrics by
GEORGE GERSHWIN
and IRA GERSHWIN

TONIGHT'S THE NIGHT

Words by
IRA GERSHWIN and GUS KAHN

Music by
GEORGE GERSHWIN

I GOT RHYTHM

Music and Lyrics by
GEORGE GERSHWIN
and IRA GERSHWIN

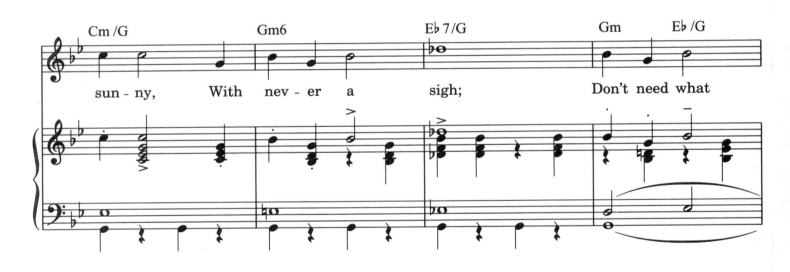

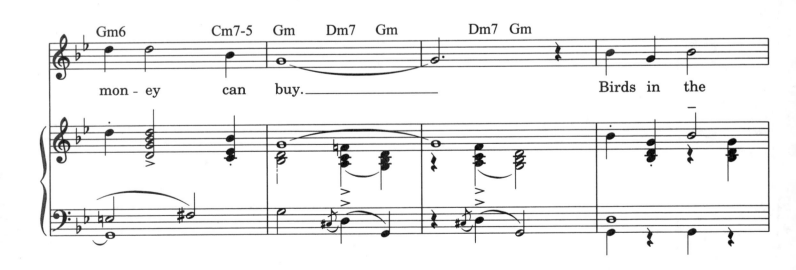

THE REAL AMERICAN FOLK SONG
(IS A RAG)

Music and Lyrics by
GEORGE GERSHWIN
and IRA GERSHWIN

Allegretto

Near Bar - ce - lo - na the peas - ant croons the
You may dis - like, or you may a - dore, the

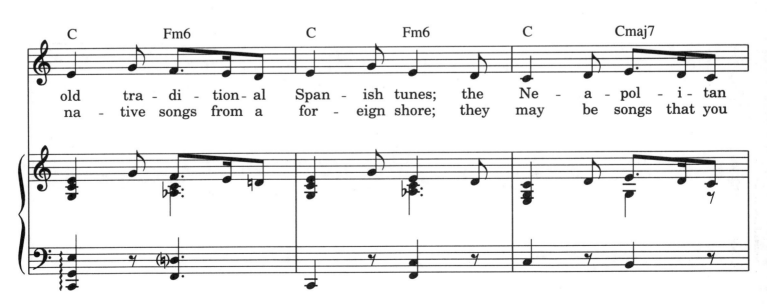

old tra - di - tion - al Span - ish tunes; the Ne - a - pol - i - tan
na - tive songs from a for - eign shore; they may be songs that you

own pe - cu - liar way. A - mer - i - can folk__ songs, I
leave the rest to fate. A rag - gy re - frain__ an - y -

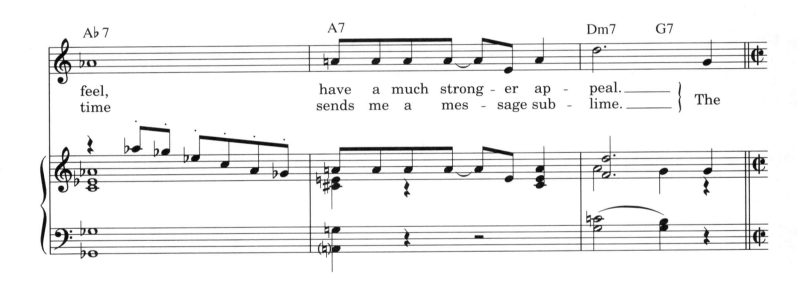

feel, have a much strong - er ap - peal.____ The
time sends me a mes - sage sub - lime.____

Refrain -
Tempo di Fox Trot

real A - mer - i - can folk song is a rag,____

WHAT CAUSES THAT?

Music and Lyrics by
GEORGE GERSHWIN
and IRA GERSHWIN

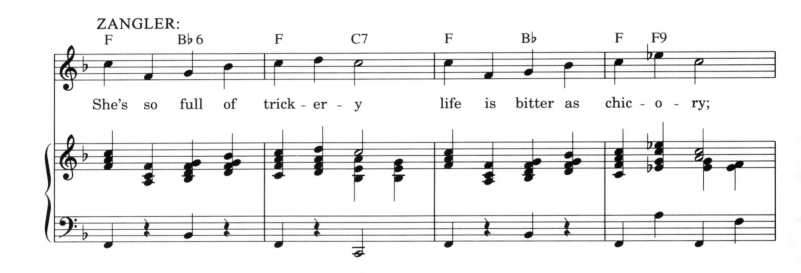

ZANGLER:

She's so full of trick-er-y life is bitter as chic-o-ry;

BOBBY:

bit-ter-ness fills my cup. I'm sor-ry you brought that up.

NAUGHTY BABY

Music and Lyrics by
GEORGE GERSHWIN,
IRA GERSHWIN and DESMOND CARTER

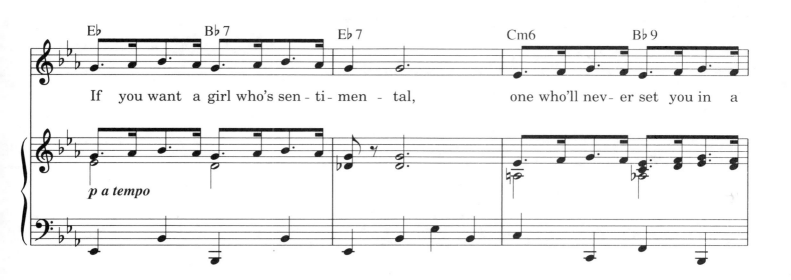

If you want a girl who's sen-ti-men-tal, one who'll nev-er set you in a

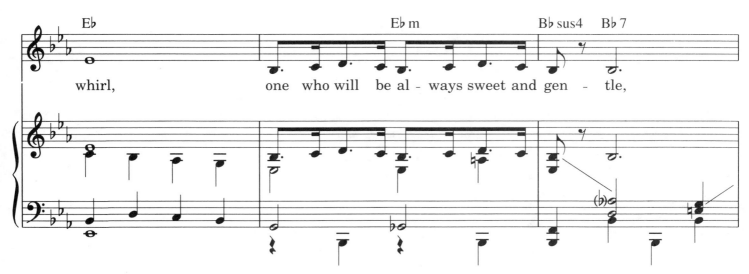

whirl, one who will be al-ways sweet and gen-tle,

I am not that sort of girl. But if you pre-fer a ra-ther

swift one, if you think you'd like to run a-round

with a bright one I am just the right

one. Naugh-ty ba - by, naugh-ty ba - by, who will tease
(2nd Time) Naugh-ty ba - by, naugh-ty ba - by, we a - dore

* 1st Time - Solo
2nd Time - Everyone

me.

I'm the sort of girl you might ex-pect to flirt with ev-'ry fel-low that she knew;

just the sort your moth-er would ob-ject to if she saw me out with you. But I al-ways do the things I want to.

STIFF UPPER LIP

Music and Lyrics by
GEORGE GERSHWIN
and IRA GERSHWIN

Moderately

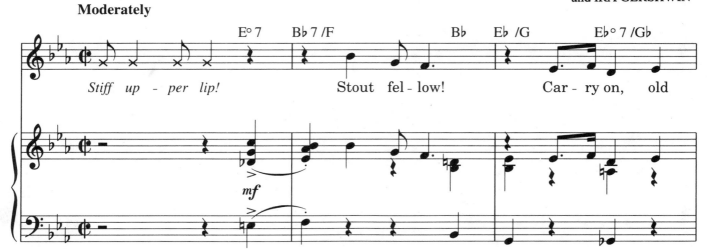

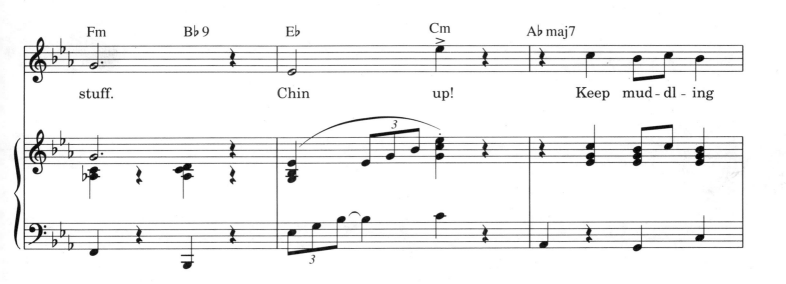

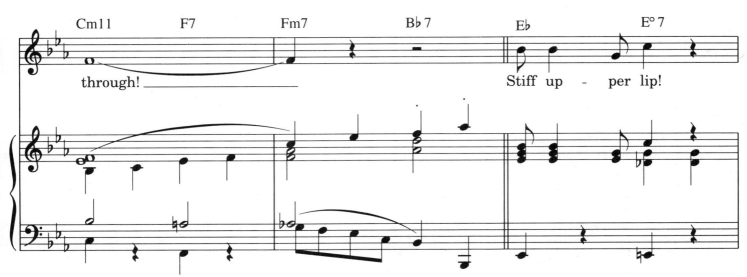

THEY CAN'T TAKE THAT AWAY FROM ME

Music and Lyrics by
GEORGE GERSHWIN
and IRA GERSHWIN

BUT NOT FOR ME

Music and Lyrics by
GEORGE GERSHWIN
and IRA GERSHWIN

Moderato

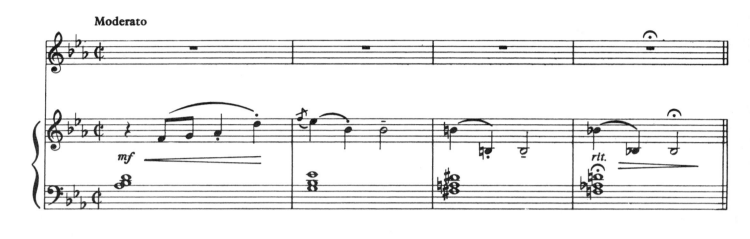

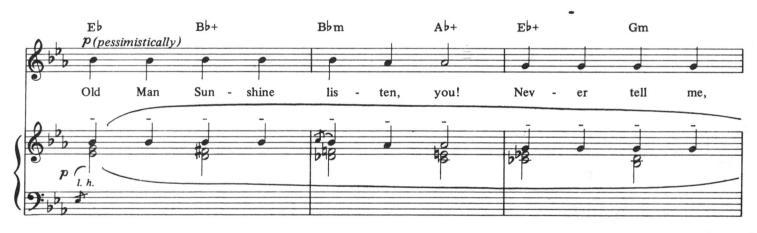

Old Man Sun - shine lis - ten, you! Nev - er tell me,

"Dreams come true!" Just try it And I'll start a ri - ot.___

NICE WORK IF YOU CAN GET IT

Music and Lyrics by
GEORGE GERSHWIN
and IRA GERSHWIN

The man who on-ly lives for mak-ing mon-ey   Lives   a   life that is-n't

nec-es-sa-ri-ly sun-ny.   Like-wise the man   who   works   for   fame,

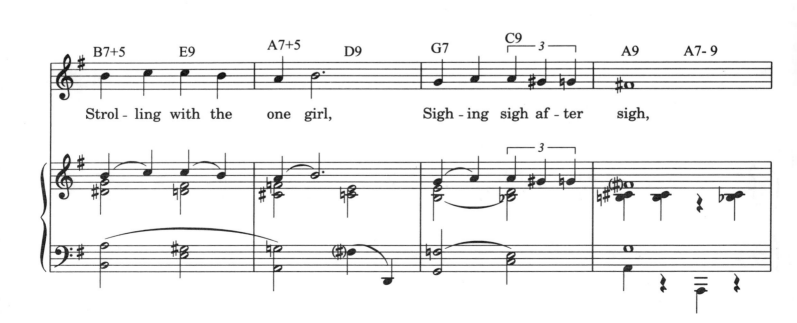

Nice Work If You Can Get It, And you can get it if you try.

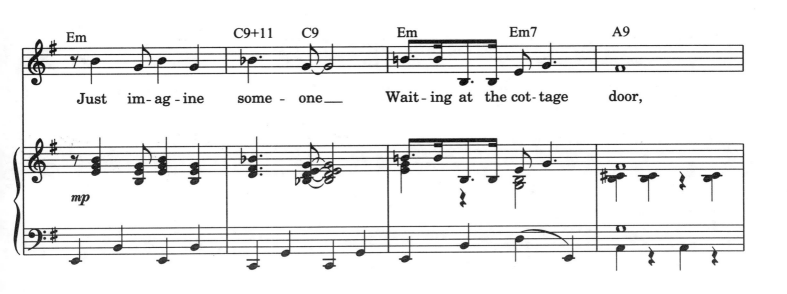

Just im-ag-ine some - one Wait-ing at the cot-tage door,

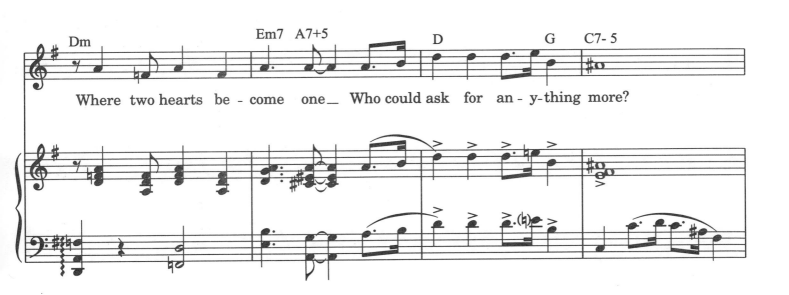

Where two hearts be - come one Who could ask for an - y-thing more?

Lov - ing one who loves you, And then tak - ing that vow,

Nice Work __ If You Can Get It, And if you get it, _____ Won't you tell me

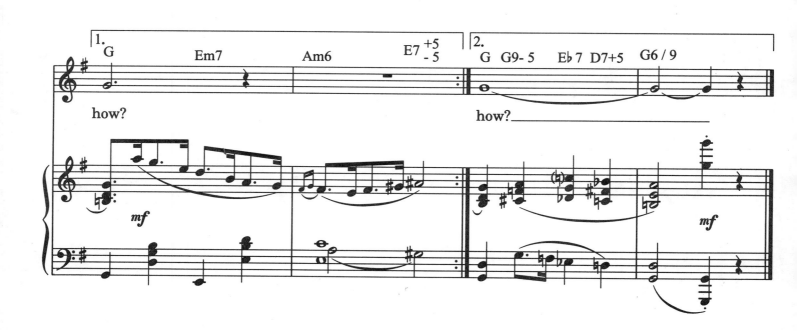

1. how?

2. how? _____